Devotions from a Hunting, Fishing, and Sports Father to His Son

Devotions from a Hunting, Fishing, and Sports Father to His Son

Gary Miller

CrossBooks™
A Division of LifeWay
1663 Liberty Drive
Bloomington, IN 47403
www.crossbooks.com
Phone: 1-866-879-0502

First published by CrossBooks 4/18/2012

ISBN: 978-1-4627-1545-9 (sc)
ISBN: 978-1-4627-1544-2 (e)

Library of Congress Control Number: 2012906235

Printed in the United States of America

Devotions from a Hunting, Fishing, Sports Father, to His Son, is simply as the title reveals. It contains fifty-two spiritual lessons shared from the wisdom and experiences of a sportsman father into the life of his maturing son.

Acknowledgements

Special thanks again to Carol Borneman and Linda Lankford. Their volunteer work and friendship is priceless. I have seen my wife's faith grow in the past few years as I have pursued the ministry of speaking and writing. We have stepped into the unknown together and have found it to be the place where God mostly dwells.

Dedication

As strange as it may seem, this book is dedicated to my two daughters, Bethany and Brittany. Over the years they have watched and laughed at my clumsiness as I tried to understand the opposite sex. They saw how awkward it was for me to try to do things that only women truly understood. They saw how unnatural it was for me to know what to buy as a birthday gift or how to "join in" with the girls. They were also keenly aware of how easy it was for me to know exactly what to do with my only son.

You may criticize my honesty, and I am not saying I did not make mistakes, but the truth still remains that boys understand boys better than boys understand girls – and the opposite is true as well. Therefore, this dedication to my girls is because they acknowledged this human and healthy difference early in life and loved me and their brother anyway.

Introduction

The bond that a father has with his son can only be known by fathers who have sons. When that relationship is not strained by the inability to get along, it is a truly blessed union. This describes my relationship with my only son, Stuart. This doesn't mean that we are close friends because that would not be an accurate description or a healthy relationship. But it does mean that he has grown up with a father who was passionate about all kinds of sports and who loved to hunt and fish. These things were all I knew, but I believed if I could introduce him to these same passions he would not only love these activities as well, but they would serve as ways to teach him the greater lessons of the Christian life.

I was right. As he grew up, he was drawn to these same passions that I believe every son is drawn to. He became a good basketball player and also loved the outdoors. This really helped me as a father because I knew just what to buy him for birthdays and Christmas. There was never a bad time to receive a knife, camping equipment, or a new gun.

As he got older his desire got stronger, even through college. Soon he would not only graduate, but leave the safe confines of my home. My desire was to give him something that would serve as a reference for his spiritual life; something that could teach a lesson in a way that he would understand. This book was my answer. It contains fifty-two of the greatest spiritual lessons I have ever learned, related through what I know and love – hunting, fishing, and sports. Some of these truths I am still learning. These devotions are meant to provide answers, encouragement, and help as he goes through the difficult early years of his adult life. But many of them are lessons that he has heard from me when he was a young child or teenager.

So this book is for the son who is eight or eighteen. It is written so that a father can read one of the devotions to his son at bedtime or so that he can give the book to his older son as a gift. The vocabulary is purposefully meant to cause the ten year old to ask his dad the meaning of some words or to be easily understood by the twenty year old without it seeming too childlike.

If you are giving it to your son as a gift, the following page is yours. Write your own special message to your son. It's easy to do. Just relate it to one of your hunting or fishing trips and he will understand. --Gary

Dear Son,

_______________________________ Dad

Psalm 78

[4] We will not hide these truths from our children; we
will tell the next generation about the glorious deeds of
the Lord, about his power and his mighty wonders.
[5] For he issued his laws to Jacob; he gave his instructions
to Israel. He commanded our ancestors to teach them to
their children,
[6] so the next generation might know them— even the
children not yet born— and they in turn will teach their
own children.
[7] So each generation should set its hope anew on
God, not forgetting his glorious miracles and obeying
his commands.
[8] Then they will not be like their ancestors— stubborn,
rebellious, and unfaithful, refusing to give their hearts to
God.

Following God

> *John 8:*[12]*Jesus said to the people, "I am the light of the world. If you follow me, you won't be stumbling through the darkness, because you will have the light that leads to life."*

Son, do you remember when I took you wading at the lake? I took you to a special place. It's special because the water recedes during the winter allowing the fish to bunch up together. We couldn't get to this particular spot with a boat so you put on your first pair of hip boots. You were a young teenager so I took you to this area knowing that you would not be quickly bored. We took my truck to the lake's edge, put on our waders, grabbed our fishing gear, and eased out into the water. As we made our way into the lake, I would begin to feel with my feet to make sure there were no rocks, logs, or deep areas underneath the water where we could not see. I would move from side to side maneuvering around any obstacle until we reached our destination. My words to you were to simply stay close behind, move where I move, and step where I step. You didn't know where we were going or how to get there, but you followed me every step of the way. You probably didn't know how to verbalize it, but you trusted me.

That's the way you have lived your life with me. You have trusted me to care for you and protect you even when you thought I didn't know what I was doing. And sometimes I probably didn't. You trusted me however, because you knew that I loved you.

As you grow in your Christian life, you will be asked to follow God in the same way. There will be many times that He will simply say, "Follow Me." He may or may not tell you where you are going and the way He takes you may seem awkward, crooked, and even slow. But remember that He loves you and that He sees things that you do not. And if you will trust Him like you did me He will lead you to places greater than you and I have ever been.

Prayer: "Lord, I know You love my son and want the very best for him. Give him the strength to follow You wherever You lead."

God's Purpose in Creation

Rom 1:[20]*From the time the world was created, people have seen the earth and sky and all that God made. They can clearly see his invisible qualities—his eternal power and divine nature. So they have no excuse whatsoever for not knowing God.*

Son, even before God made man, He created this world and the earth we live on. He created the mountains and the oceans. He created the valleys and the plains. He created the trees and animals. All of this was done at His word and by His hand. Some may have formed by floods or earthquakes but even these were guided by God. I don't understand it all but I've been in the woods and on the water long enough to know that someone bigger than your dad created it.

You and I get to enjoy much of His creation every time we go outside. When we go hunting or fishing we get to see things that God created. What you need to remember however, is that nothing He created was by chance. He had a purpose in everything. God didn't just create something because it sounded like a good idea. He had a plan.

Today's Scripture says that through all that God created we can see "*His invisible qualities, His eternal power, and His divine nature.*" This means that all of creation will point you to God and will let you know something about Him. That's why it's important to learn about nature, because as you learn about nature, you will also learn about God. I'll share some of these examples in the days ahead. But for now, each time you go outside, ask God to show you something about Himself through His creation.

Prayer: "God, cause my son to know more about Your creation, so he will know more about You."

Man: God's Greatest Creation

Gen. 2:[7] And the LORD God formed a man's body from the dust of the ground and breathed into it the breath of life. And the man became a living person.

Gen 1:[28] God blessed them and told them, "Multiply and fill the earth and subdue it. Be masters over the fish and birds and all the animals."

Son, God's greatest creations were man and woman. They were greater and more special than any other of His creations. The Bible says that God "*breathed into it the breath of life.*" We are the only creation that God breathed this "life" into. Other creations have life and breath but the life that He gave us was unique. He made us in *His* likeness and told us to be masters over all the other animals on the earth. He put them here for us, to meet our needs and for us to manage and care for. Some of His creations are given to us for food, some we have as pets, and others help us keep nature in balance.

It's very important that you respect all animals, even the ones that you kill for food, clothing, and sport. It's also important that you remember that you are to be good managers of all the animals here on earth. In the Bible, David had to kill a bear and a lion because they were killing his sheep. It was necessary in order for him to keep his flock safe. He was being a good manager of what God had given him. That's why farmers want rid of coyotes, groundhogs, and even wild hogs. They destroy what the farmer tries to manage. That's why the owners of the places we hunt want us to kill them. Just don't eat em'.

Son, you are a living person. You are God's prize creation because you have within you the breath of God. You have also been given the responsibility of managing all other created things. Hunting and fishing are great privileges that you have but you must make sure that you stay within the laws of each state and the laws made by God. You have a great responsibility to both.

Prayer: "Lord, help my son be a good manager of Your creation and to keep the laws of man and God."

The Truth of an Acorn

John 12:[24]The truth is, a kernel of wheat must be planted in the soil. Unless it dies it will be alone—a single seed. But its death will produce many new kernels—a plentiful harvest of new lives.

Son, a favorite food of deer is acorns. In autumn, they fall from oak trees onto the ground where deer gobble them up. Try to find a white oak tree that's bearing acorns and set your tree stand up there. With patience you will be successful.

Some years there are so many acorns that the deer can't eat them all. God plans it this way. In order for more oak trees to grow there have to be acorns left uneaten. You see, acorns are the seeds of an oak tree. If left alone, many of them will get buried in the leaves and dirt. They will lay dormant for a period of time and then will begin to sprout. A tiny plant will break through the acorn and will produce a new oak tree that could grow to be hundreds of years old. The next time you're in the woods move away the leaves from beneath an oak tree and you'll find an acorn that is giving new life.

The acorn is another way that God will show you about Himself through nature. It will give you another picture of Jesus' death, burial, and resurrection. You see the acorn points to this same thing. It falls to the ground away from the tree. It is buried beneath the dirt and leaves and thought for dead. But in a little while it will burst open with a new resurrected life.

It is the same for Christians. Death is not the end. It is the start of a new beginning and a new life in Heaven, where we will live forever. And just as Jesus was raised from the dead, we too will be one day.

Prayer: “God, lead my son to constantly find spiritual truths through Your creation.”

Wanting What's Best for You

Matt. 7: [9]You parents—if your children ask for a loaf of bread, do you give them a stone instead? [10]Or if they ask for a fish, do you give them a snake? Of course not! [11]If you sinful people know how to give good gifts to your children, how much more will your heavenly Father give good gifts to those who ask him.

Son, I can remember your first fishing trip and your first fish. I still have the picture of you standing there with rod held high, a small bluegill on the end of your line, your snoopy rod, and nothing on but a tank top and your snoopy underwear. What a great day for you and me.

I know you remember that day even though you were very young. Do you remember how your mom and I, and your sisters, were so happy and how we celebrated with you? Those days are as great for me as they are for you. I want to rejoice with you. As you get older I will continue to do the same. It may show up in hugs and kisses no matter how old you may be, or it may show up in high-fives or just a smile or wink. But I really do feel a great sense of pleasure when you accomplish something – anything.

I also hurt when you hurt. I feel the pain that you feel when you strike out or miss the winning basket or never catch a fish. You are a great treasure that God has given me and I want the very best for you.

In an even greater way, God desires the very best for you as well. You are His child. He hurts when you hurt. He feels your pain and disappointment. And He also rejoices when you achieve great things.

As you grow up there will be things that happen that you don't understand. There will be disappointments and failure. When these things happen, remember this verse. It will encourage you to know how much God really thinks about you.

Prayer: "Thank You God that You want the best for my son. Teach him to trust You even when things don't go as planned."

Be Thankful

I Thessalonians 5: [18]No matter what happens always be thankful, for this is God's will for you who belong to Christ Jesus.

Son, God has a plan for you. As you get older you will discover that plan. It's very important that you allow God to show it to you. It will cause your life to be full and complete. I don't know how wealthy you may be or what kind of position you may hold but neither of these will bring inner fulfillment. Being in God's will however, doesn't just mean that He has an overall plan for you. It means being led by Him each day. Your greatest days will be when you know you are doing the will of God.

I know how you can do that. Our Bible verse for today says *"No matter what happens always be thankful, for THIS IS THE WILL OF GOD!"* If you want to be in God's will each day, make thankfulness a priority. You will have to practice it until it becomes natural, but that will come.

The art of being thankful will lie in your ability to see the little things. Don't just be thankful for unexpected blessings but learn to find things to be thankful for. God didn't give us certain things to thank Him for, but "in all things."

Let me give you some ideas. Thank Him for your eyes that allow you to see His creation; your ears that let you hear the footsteps of that big buck. Thank Him for being able to smell the aroma of the lake. Thank Him for the big things like your home, truck, health, job, wife, and kids – whenever you may have these. Thank Him also for the little things, like your camping gear, shotgun, boots, Ipod, an air-conditioned room, a TV, and even your pocket knife. Thank Him for your church, friends, family, and especially for sending His Son, Jesus.

There will come days that you will struggle in your spiritual life. During those times, muster up all that is within you, and begin to give thanks. You will move quickly into the perfect will of God.

Prayer: "Lord, teach my son early in life to become thankful. Let him see it in me."

Be Kind

Ephesians 4: [32]Instead, be kind to each other, tenderhearted, forgiving one another, just as God through Christ has forgiven you.

Son, you know I've always loved the outdoors and other sports as well. You were raised on ESPN. I thought about naming you that. I watched you as you grew into a little athlete. I noticed that God had even gifted you in certain areas. I new I had to make sure that you handled success with spiritual integrity.

Many people who have become successful do not know how to handle it. They are quick to praise themselves and to look at others as lesser individuals. They become prideful and God hates this.

Always remember that God has gifted each one of us differently and just because someone may not be as good as you in a certain area, they are better than you in another. To look down on them is to not recognize this truth. That's why you should never laugh at another player's inability or fuss at someone who can simply not do what you may be able to do. Remember that God has given them other gifts and they are as important as you are. Be kind. I know you may not see a lot of kindness in this world, but it still doesn't give you permission to be otherwise. Everyone deserves kindness, no matter what color, creed, or condition. And make sure you treat the opposite sex with extreme kindness. You may not receive it and your kindness may not be appreciated by some, but it is the right thing to do.

Prayer: "Lord, give my son the spirit of kindness and make me kinder as well."

Guard Your Heart and Your Gun Will be Fine

> *Mark 7:*[21]*For from within, out of a person's heart, come evil thoughts, sexual immorality, theft, murder,* [22]*adultery, greed, wickedness, deceit, eagerness for lustful pleasure, envy, slander, pride, and foolishness.* [23]*All these vile things come from within; they are what defile you and make you unacceptable to God."*

Son, a lot of folks don't understand people who hunt and fish. To them we are unlearned and barbaric (sort of like a caveman). They think that we just go out and kill stuff and have no heart or feelings toward animals. Some will even go out of their way to make all hunting illegal. What's funny is they think if I have a gun in my home, that I'm an irresponsible parent. Most of the time, you will not be able to convince these people any different. It won't matter how fair you are or how kind you are to them, or even how educated you are, they will still spew out hateful and mostly ignorant points of view.

For some reason many people think that a good citizen surely would not own a gun and that we must live with some sort of uneasy fear about the environment we live in. They only say that because they have never known our lifestyle.

Ever since you were born, you have witnessed some type of gun in our house. I used the same principles that I used with everything else, to teach you about dangerous things.....Don't stick any object in an electrical outlet, it could kill you. Don't play with matches, you could burn the house down and someone could die. Don't drink anything that you're not sure what it is. It could kill you. Don't take anything that's in the medicine cabinet, it could kill you. And don't play with guns. Someone could die.

It really wasn't brain surgery. You understood that that there are many things in this world that could cause great harm, but each one is also a tool and some are even essential to our lives.

The truth is, bad people will always find a way to do bad things and good people will find a way to do good things. Being good or bad does not come from what we hold in our hands but what we hold dear in our heart. Make sure that your heart is right with God and then whatever you hold in your hands will be used for good – whether it's a dollar or a gun.

Prayer: "Lord, teach my son to love even those who don't understand him, and to have a right heart."

You Are a Boy

I Samuel 1:[20]And in due time she gave birth to a son. She named him Samuel, for she said, "I asked the LORD for him."

Son, a man was built for adventure. God planted this trait within us. It is very natural for you to be rough, to like dirt, and to flex your muscles. Boys fight and get into trouble more than girls. God made us physically stronger than them as well. He made us risk takers. There's something within our spirit that makes us want to excel. Most all outdoor discoveries and accomplishments first came by a man. This doesn't mean that we are better than females, only different.

You have a desire within you to be outdoors. It's almost like something is drawing you to be out in God's creation. The truth is we are drawn to the outdoors because it embodies all of those things that make boys different from girls. The lessons that you learn there will be lived out at home. You will learn about patience, protection, and provision. You will learn that you can endure tough times, that you can do without a lot of things, and that you can live from the land. You will learn to fight the elements and conquer the circumstances. These lessons will be valuable reminders as you become the husband and father that God wants you to be.

At home, your job will be to protect and provide for your family. You will fight for them if necessary. You will sacrifice your own needs for the ones you are sent to protect. But God is getting you ready. So keep hanging from those trees. Keep camping with your friends. Don't be concerned if you run out of food, or if it rains on you, or if you happen across a snake. You may come back with a few scars and maybe even a broken arm or two, but one day these will be proud battle scars for a man who grew up just like God wanted him to.

Prayer: "God, thank You for my young man and for the spirit of adventure that You have placed inside of him."

From Father to Friend

Deuteronomy 1:[31]And you saw how the LORD your God cared for you again and again here in the wilderness, just as a father cares for his child.

Son, I am your father. I want to be your friend. I long to be your friend, but the role God has given me right now is to be your father. If your teacher were to ask you to make a list of your friends, I would not be on the list. It's okay. You don't view me as a friend. I'm your father. I'm your daddy.

A father has a greater responsibility than a friend. To be your father means that I have to get you ready for manhood. I have to protect and provide for you. Sometimes I don't like what I have to do but it's part of the job. I have to make decisions that you are not going to like sometimes. It doesn't mean that I love you less. In fact, it means I love you more because I can't do what I want to do. I have to do what's best for you. That doesn't mean that I'm *not* your friend. It just means that being your friend has to come just below being your father.

One day my role will be complete in its function. That is, I will still be your father by title, but my task will be done. You will then be a man with your own family and perhaps your own son. That's when you will have to be a father and then I can be your friend. I can't wait for that day!

Prayer: "God help me be a father to my son first, and a friend second."

Wait on God

Psalm 37: [7]Be still in the presence of the LORD, and wait patiently for him to act.

Son, it's really fun to catch bass on top water bait, but if you're going to be successful you have to *wait* until you feel the fish on your line. If you try setting the hook when you *see* the fish hit it, you will miss. You have to fight what you see and what you think and the urgency of the moment. I've watched you learn this technique of waiting and you have enjoyed the thrill of a fighting fish.

Waiting on God will be one of the most important parts of your Christian life, maybe the most important. The circumstances around you will put a lot of pressure on you to act. You will think God is not listening, you can't hear Him, or that He doesn't really care about what you do. But He knows everything and His timing is always perfect. He is never in a hurry, is never caught off guard, and can speak loudly and clearly enough for you to hear. Waiting is not inactivity. It is very active, but the activity involves seeking His word on this matter through prayer and searching the Scriptures. And nothing is too small to take to Him. Whether it's buying a car, a house, getting a job, or anything else, seek God's direction and wait for Him to answer.

God makes us wait in order to build our faith in Him and to keep us out of trouble – remember, He knows things that we don't know. You will eliminate a whole lot of headaches in your life if you will learn this. Don't budge until God gives you the go-ahead and you will enjoy the fruit of this kind of lesson as well.

Prayer: "Lord, show my son early in life, the benefit of waiting on You. It will serve him well his entire life."

Don't Be a Lazy Hunter

Proverbs 12:[27]Lazy people don't even cook the game they catch, but the diligent make use of everything they find.

Son, some of the biggest smiles that I've ever seen come across your face were when you made a good shot on a deer. I can remember your first bow kill. You had already dragged it out before I had even gotten out of the woods. I know that took a lot of strength and effort. I was very proud of you. Sometimes it will take hours to get an animal from where it dies, to your truck. You will be responsible to do whatever it takes to get that job done. There's a saying in the hunting world that says, "The work starts after the kill." This is so true, as you have experienced. Most experts say in deer hunting that you will need three hours from the shot to your recliner. If you can't give that, then let it walk.

Our Bible verse today says, *"Lazy people don't even cook the game they catch."* You can't be that way. If you don't eat it, find someone to give your game to. Don't just leave it lie. And when you're fishing, either turn them loose or take them home and clean them. This is not only good ethics (right thing to do according to the world), but it is also the right thing to do according the Lord. When you're helping the landowners get rid of the coyotes and ground hogs, this doesn't apply, and God is okay with that as well.

If you will do this, you will sleep well at night, not only from the work, but from the peace of mind.

Prayer: "Lord, teach my son to be a good hunter and fisherman, one that is pleasing to You and to his fellow man."

Pay Attention to the Clouds

Nahum 1:[3]*...He displays his power in the whirlwind and the storm. The billowing clouds are the dust beneath his feet.*

Son, there will be many times that you will find yourself outdoors. You may be fishing or just camping. I want you to notice the clouds. They are put there by God to tell you something about Him. Remember, God's creation will always tell you something about Him.

You may travel to many places in your life. All of these places will have their unique characteristics. Some will have high mountains and some wide valleys. Some will have flat land and others rolling hills. One thing that is common in all parts of the world is clouds. Some areas have more than others, but all will have some. God put them in the sky where everyone can see. They will remind you of His presence. They are the footprints of God. As our Bible verse says, they are *"the dust of His feet."*

As you hunt and fish, you will travel many dusty roads in your truck. If someone is behind you they will know you've been there. If you drive into the dust, someone is up ahead. The clouds above you will let you know that God has just been there. They will give you a physical picture of the surety of His presence. This will be important to you as you go through life. Sometimes it will seem that God is absent. You will call to Him and it will seem like He's nowhere to be found. The clouds will be an encouragement to you during those times. No matter where you are, you will always be able to look up and see that He is watching over you even when you can't feel Him or sense Him. You may have to look far away to find a stray cloud at times, but I'm sure when you *need* to see one, there will be one right above you.

Prayer: "Lord, constantly remind my son about Your constant presence through Your clouds."

Follow Me as I Follow Christ

Philippians 4: [9]Keep putting into practice all you learned from me and heard from me and saw me doing, and the God of peace will be with you.-- Paul

Son, since I have always loved the outdoors and many other sports, you have had to follow me. And even though you will follow your own path one day, it's good to know that much of what I like, you do to. You especially love fishing, camping, and basketball. I'm thankful that I have been able to guide you in things from shooting a basketball to shooting a bow.

You have also taught me a lot – especially about how important my example is to you and your sisters. You children seem to keep us parents in check.

My greatest desire has been to show you by example, how to live the Christian life. I've failed many times but even in failure there are right ways to respond to that as well. Whether I realize it or not you're watching me and even though there are different ways to catch a fish, there's only one way to live the Christian life. I need to make sure I'm doing it the right way. I figure if Paul was willing to set himself up as an example for the Philippian church, then you ought to be able to learn the Christian life from me. That's why I study the Bible. There's a lot of you riding on me.

There are a lot of people looking at you as well. That's why you too must set the right example in your Christian life. One day your boy will follow you, so make sure that you get this right now. That way you won't make as many mistakes when he's watching.

Prayer: "Lord, help me to be like You, because my son wants to be like me."

Learn From the Trees

Psalm 96: [12]*Let the fields and their crops burst forth with joy! Let the trees of the forest rustle with praise before the Lord!*

Son, if you're going to spend a lot of time outdoors, you need to learn how to identify some trees. You can't deer hunt if you don't know the difference between a white oak and a maple. Now there are still some that I can't recognize, but I do know most. During most of our trips in the woods I have tried to give you a little information on certain ones, but as you get older, you will need to educate yourself. This will serve you well your whole life.

Even though you need to know about these trees for hunting purposes, you also need to look at them with your spiritual eyes. Trees will remind you to constantly give praise to God.

When you look at a tree, each one looks as if they are raising their hands (limbs) to God. And even though many limbs must grow around rocks, and fences, and other obstacles, they still find a way to reach up to the heavens. Our Bible verse today says that these trees *"rustle with praise before the Lord."*

There will be times of difficulty and pain in your life but you must find a way to praise God in and around these obstacles, because God loves praise.

Praise is like being thankful except in praise we are recognizing God for things that are not just for us. You see I can thank God for my new knife, but I praise God for a beautiful tree. A tree is for everyone and just helps me remember the greatness of God. Always praise God for particular parts of His Creation. When you do this you will see His greatness and realize if He can create something as awesome as this earth, He surely can take care of you.

Prayer: "Lord, help my son see the beauty in a tree and praise You for Your greatness."

About Women

Proverbs 31: [10]Who can find a virtuous and capable wife? She is worth more than precious rubies. [11]Her husband can trust her, and she will greatly enrich his life. [12]She will not hinder him but help him all her life.

Son, girls are great! Your sisters came along before you did and they are so special – and so different. God made them beautiful with skin so perfect. They were meant to hug and kiss and dress up. And even though they play sports, they clean up a lot better than we do. Let's face it, we need them and want them in our lives. A man is really not complete without women in his life.

The world that you live in now is different from when I was young. Some things are better and some things are not. But I want to remind you to always cherish the women in your life, whether it's your mother, your sisters, or your wife. They really do most of the work in our society. They pretty much run the home and many will work outside the home as well. And then to beat it all, they have the babies. They are God's best creation. Because they are so precious, you need to treat them that way. Opening doors for them and giving them your seat is a must. And you have to be willing to do the heavy stuff. We surely don't want them getting hurt. Always, always recognize their great worth.

One day, you will get married. You will choose a beautiful girl. Make sure that she never doubts how much you love her. Heap praises on her publically and privately. Guard her, provide for her, and protect her as your most precious gift from God. If you do this, she will honor you as well and make your life full. Gifts are good, but she wants to hear words come from your mouth. She wants to see it in your eyes and feel it in your hugs. Don't disappoint her and she will be a blessing to you for all your life.

Prayer: "Lord, cause my son to understand the great worth of the women in his life."

You Need Others

I Corinthians 12: [18]But God made our bodies with many parts, and he has put each part just where he wants it. [19]What a strange thing a body would be if it had only one part! [20]Yes, there are many parts, but only one body. [21]The eye can never say to the hand, "I don't need you." The head can't say to the feet, "I don't need you."

Son, you know I love to bow hunt. It's my favorite way to hunt deer. There's just something about being able to hunt similar to our ancestors. And it's a lot more challenging. You have also experienced drawing on a deer with your bow. You have felt your heart beat so fast that you were unsure if you were going to be able to make the shot. But you did, and were successful.

The bow is a fined tuned piece of equipment. However, the bow needs other parts like a sight and a rest if it is to accomplish what it was built for. If just one part of it is not adjusted correctly or is missing, the shot will be off.

As you become a man, you will discover the purpose that God has for you. This purpose will always involve other people. You will not accomplish the plans God has for you alone. Just as a basketball team needs all five players carrying out their role, you will also find that in your calling, you will have a role that involves others. You must value each member of your team. Each one of you will be part of something that one individual could not accomplish themselves. Some may hold a position that seems larger than another, like being the bow, and some positions might be small like the bow sight. But without both, neither will be able to do what it was created to do. Working together will not only help each of you to accomplish your individual purpose, but it will also produce something bigger than either of you could ever imagine.

Prayer: "Lord, help my son see the worth of teamwork."

Disappointments and Discouragement

Philippians 4:[8] And now, dear brothers and sisters, let me say one more thing as I close this letter. Fix your thoughts on what is true and honorable and right. Think about things that are pure and lovely and admirable. Think about things that are excellent and worthy of praise.

Son, disappointment and discouragement are two different things. I know you have gone through both, but disappointments will come more frequently especially if you expect a lot – and you should. Disappointments come a whole lot when you hunt and fish. I've never went fishing or hunting expecting not to bring home game, but most of the time I come home empty-handed. I am disappointed. Ballgames bring disappointment when you don't do as good as you wanted to or when you lose. Life is full of disappointments. Get use to it and then get over it.

Discouragement is another thing. Discouragement means the loss of courage. It means that you have come to a period in your life where it seems that a certain situation will never be made right, and you have lost hope. This is something you must deal with spiritually.

You see, if you are constantly looking at the circumstances and the situations your emotions will go where they go. That's why people are down in the dumps on one day and excited on the next. We are to set our eyes on Jesus. Our Bible verse also tells us to set them on the good things in life. When we set our eyes on Christ, we are fixing them on something or Someone that does not change. Circumstances change. Christ doesn't. And as our faith grows in Him, we will go through less and less periods of discouragement. You must choose daily to keep your eyes fixed on your God who does not change, has everything in control, and knows every detail about the situation that you are in. The more you read God's word the more faith and courage you will have that God will work out everything in your life for His good.

Prayer: Father, let both of us have courage in You, because You never change.

Learn to be Still

Psalm 131:[1]LORD, my heart is not proud; my eyes are not haughty. I don't concern myself with matters too great or awesome for me. [2]But I have stilled and quieted myself, just as a small child is quiet with its mother. Yes, like a small child is my soul within me.

Son, we both love to hunt and fish. My best times have been with you. And as you know, I have always rather you catch more fish than me. But there is something about this outdoor life that is difficult for youngsters. It's being quiet. I was always sort of glad when you went to sleep when we were deer hunting. I knew that you would be still and quiet. As you get older, this will come more easily.

When I was young I had the same problem. Being still and quiet were not part of who I was. I was always known as the one that was full of energy and never stopped. Even as a young adult I had to be going all the time. I'm not that way now and hunting and fishing have helped me in becoming this way.

In your spiritual life you must learn to be still and quiet. These are the times that God speaks more often and more clearly. This will be crucial to every other part of your life. You must learn to take time to be quiet with God. It takes coming away from your activities. It takes getting to a place that has no interruptions and allowing God to speak to you in the quietness and stillness of your time there. It can't be rushed or you will miss some very important information that God wants to tell you. You will have prayers that you want answered. You will have directions that you need God to guide you in. You will need to see what God wants from you. But these will only come as you learn to be still and quiet in His presence.

During these times, bring your Bible, a small notebook, and a pen. Come expecting God to meet you there. Do your talking to God, then let Him do His talking to you. He will speak to you through His word and into your spirit. And you will know all you need to know to face the day with confidence.

Prayer: "Father, teach my son the benefits of sitting before You in quietness."

The Wilderness

Luke 1:[80] John grew up and became strong in spirit. Then he lived out in the wilderness until he began his public ministry to Israel.

Son, I have always enjoyed time away, alone. I have been drawn by the Lord, at times, to come away and spend a few days with Him. Early on, your mother didn't understand my need to leave for a couple of days. During those times I never told her why I had to go. After a few years, she understood. I also think it's a man-thing but I know that not every man gets to do it. I'm not sure how often you will, but I wanted to tell you about its benefits.

I learned a few years ago that some of the greatest men in the Bible spent time in the wilderness. Moses, Paul, Elijah, and Jesus Himself were drawn to this extended time alone with God. John the Baptist lived most of his adult life there and Jesus said there was no one greater than him. I can tell you it is time well spent.

It takes more than one day on these types of trips. It usually takes at least one day for my mind to leave civilization before it can focus on why I'm there. Most of the time, these trips were free of TV, internet, cell phones, and the like. It was just God and me.

One day the Lord may draw you to do this. You will know when He does. It will start in your mind and work its way into your spirit until you can't ignore it any longer. Just know that when this happens, God has a special word that He needs to get to you. It will be one that you will need to chew on a while. It may be one that will trigger questions. But whatever the case, respond to His call. Everyone else will understand.

Prayer: "Father, make my son sensitive to Your call, no matter where it may lead him."

Face Your Fears

Proverbs 14:[26] Those who fear the LORD are secure; he will be a place of refuge for their children.

Son, many times hunting means arriving before daylight. That means you have to travel through the woods in the dark with just a small flashlight. I have to admit that there were times I have been a little afraid. Some places I go have bears and other ornery critters that I had rather not run into. There have also been times that I have walked through the woods when all of a sudden a screech owl let out a scream just above my head. Well, let's just say that I didn't act very manly.

Fears are real. Some fear we need to have, like don't mess with a rattlesnake and don't climb a dead tree. Other fears are unfounded and only serve to hinder us from all we can be and do. Some people fear heights, needles, and even riding in an elevator. I'm not making fun of anyone but I'm telling you to face your fears. And the way that you do that is to realize the Bible gives us one thing (person) to fear – God.

That doesn't mean that we are afraid of God, but only that we have a healthy and holy respect for who He is and that we understand that He is above everything else. What that means for you is if you will fear God you won't have to fear anything else. Again, that doesn't mean that you do stupid things because God has set in creation, laws like gravity. So if you jump off of a building you are going to get hurt. This is one of God's natural laws. But to be afraid of something that is in your normal way of life is to set your fear of a certain thing above your fear of God. Don't do that.

When you have to walk in the woods before daylight, be reminded that God is there with you. When you go to bed at night and the lights go out, don't be afraid of anything because God is above whatever is trying to scare you and He will take care of the ones who fear Him. Face your fears with God and you will do things and go places others will never get to because they have not learned what you have.

Prayer: "Father, let my son know that You are greater and stronger than anything he might ever fear."

Peace in the Middle of Pressure

Isaiah 26:[3]You will keep in perfect peace all who trust in you, whose thoughts are fixed upon you!

Son, as you grow older, your experiences will grow as well. Some of these will be good and others not so good. You will also find yourself under some kind of pressure to perform or get something done. It's sort of like having a test tomorrow that you have to pass and not knowing if you are going to make the grade you need to make. The night before that test can cause you to be overly concerned and even worried.

Other things in life will come about suddenly and you will immediately feel scared. Sometimes it will be a big decision that you must make and you're not sure which one to make. At times you will find yourself going to bed with something on your mind and waking up with it still there. And sometimes you will lose sleep.

I've experienced those things and on occasion I still do. But I found a secret in the Bible that's really not meant to be a secret. It's really a truth that you must memorize and lean on the rest of your life. It is in our Bible verse for today. You see, what we lack sometimes in these pressure situations is peace. We just don't have it and it may cause us to lose sleep. This is not God's plan. His plan is for us to take our thoughts off of our situation and "fix" them on God. When we do that, it shows that our trust is in Him.

When I learned this truth, I began to apply it when something was really bothering me. And when some problem woke me up at night, I would simply quote this verse. I never failed to fall back to sleep. He gave me peace. I don't want you to have any sleepless nights, and God doesn't either. So memorize this verse and it will be your blanket when you become an adult.

Prayer: "Father, I thank You that You have provided peace for my son that he can call on the rest of his life."

A Gobbler's Pride

Proverbs 16: [18] *Pride goes before destruction and haughtiness before a fall.*

Son, turkey hunting has been a real pleasure in my life and it will be in yours as well. I've chased these birds all over the country and have learned a whole lot as I have watched them. They are a beautiful bird that can teach you a valuable lesson.

That gobbler loves to strut his stuff, especially when he is putting on a show for the hens. He will puff up as to look bigger than he really is. He will fan his tail feathers, dance around, and gobble so loud that you can hear him all through the woods. And even though these things make for a good show, they are also what puts him on my dinner table. As our Bible verse says, *"Pride goes before destruction."* And a turkey's pride is what causes his destruction. And it will cause yours as well.

The way of a Christian is humility, not pride. Humility does not mean that you let someone mistreat you or that you have no self confidence, but it simply means that you realize privately and publically that all good things come from God and that any success that you may achieve will only be by His hand. It also means that you are slow to boast about your own achievements and are quick to recognize the achievements of others.

Another Scripture concerning this says to *"humble yourself before God and in His good time, He will honor you."* So many people today are all about honoring themselves like that gobbler. They strut their accomplishments, have a puffed up ego, and make themselves bigger than they actually are. They are loud and proud. Their destruction will come. You have to be different. Humble yourself and in God's perfect time, He will honor you in ways and in places that you could never do tooting your own horn.

Prayer: "Father, teach my son to humble himself. Help me to show him by example."

Trusting Me, Trusting God

Psalm 34:[10]Even strong young lions sometimes go hungry, but those who trust in the LORD will never lack any good thing.

Son, over the years, I hope that you have been able to put some trust in me. There's no doubt that at times I've let you down. I hope those moments have been few and that I have sought your forgiveness. Trust is so important. No relationship you will ever have will be healthy without trust. This goes for relationships between boss and employee, coach and player, husband and wife, and certainly you and God.

If you think about it, you have put a lot of trust in me all of your life. You have trusted me to provide a home, food, clothes, and to teach you how to live in this world. I have taken all of the responsibility for these things. Your part has simply been to live your life staying close to me. You have never wondered if any of these things would be there for you. You rested in the truth that I would provide for you and you didn't even know you were doing it. That's trust.

One day you will understand more about how much better all relationships are when there is trust. The most important trust area for you however, will be in your relationship with God. As your Heavenly Father, He has taken all of the responsibility for every area of your life. You don't ever need to wonder if He is able to meet every need that you have. He is. You don't ever have to worry or fret or lose sleep thinking about whether God will take care of you. He will. You will only need to stay close to Him.

The closer you are to me, the more secure you feel. It will be the same with God. You see, all of those things that you thought I provided, were actually provided by God anyway. I just tried to stay close to Him because you were more than I could handle on my own.

Prayer: "Father, teach my son that his first responsibility will be to stay close to You."

Don't Worry

Matthew 6: 25 "So I tell you, don't worry about
everyday life—whether you have enough food,
drink, and clothes. Doesn't life consist of more
than food and clothing? 26 Look at the birds. They
don't need to plant or harvest or put food in barns
because your heavenly Father feeds them. And you
are far more valuable to him than they are. 27 Can
all your worries add a single moment to your life?
Of course not.

28 "And why worry about your clothes? Look at the
lilies and how they grow. They don't work or make
their clothing, 29 yet Solomon in all his glory was
not dressed as beautifully as they are. 30 And if God
cares so wonderfully for flowers that are here today
and gone tomorrow, won't he more surely care for
you? You have so little faith!

31 "So don't worry about having enough food or
drink or clothing. 32 Why be like the pagans who
are so deeply concerned about these things? Your
heavenly Father already knows all your needs,
33 and he will give you all you need from day to day
if you live for him and make the Kingdom of God
your primary concern.

Son, there is a word that I want you to know and then forget. The word is "worry." Most people use this word in their everyday conversation. They will say things like, "I'm worried about Joe," or "I'm worried about a test," or "I'm worried about my job." These people mean well, but the Bible is very clear when it comes to worry. It says don't do it!

Many years ago, I found myself using this same language until I read today's Bible verse. It plainly says, *"Don't worry."* And it goes on to say that worry is for unbelievers, not for Christians. After reading this I decided to remove that word from my vocabulary unless I was talking about it like I am now. When I did this I began to enjoy a freedom that I had never had. It was like I was set free from the responsibilities of my own life. And I was. It was God who would be responsible for me and I never had to occupy my mind with worry any longer. That's what worry does. It occupies your mind with things that cause you to be afraid, lose sleep, and get discouraged. It occupies your mind because you are trying to figure out an answer that has not come or how to fix a problem that seems unfixable. But worry cannot do one thing for any problem. It can only cause you to take your mind off of God and put it on the problem.

As you become an adult, you will be tempted to worry about a lot of things in your life. When this happens, recognize that the devil is trying to take your mind off the ability of God and on your own inability. You will get a head start if you will learn this word and then forget it.

Prayer: "Lord, teach my son early about the sin of worry."

You Can Do It

Philippians 4:[13]*For I can do everything with the help of Christ who gives me the strength I need.*

Son, I can remember the first time you went on a real hunt. You were just seven years old. We dressed you up in camo clothes and put my hat on you after adjusting it as small as we could. And even though your shotgun was a junior model, it was still too heavy for you to hold up by yourself. I knew that if we even saw a squirrel, it would be difficult for you to aim long enough to get off a good shot. Well we brought home three that day and I still have the picture to prove it. I was never prouder.

If you remember, since you were unable to hold that gun up long enough to shoot, I decided to let you lean the barrel of it over my shoulder and rest it there long enough for you to make a good shot. Now that I look back at it, I wonder why I never just brought a shooting stick.

Those times are not over for you. In fact, there will be many times that God will ask you to do something where the task is bigger than you. You will think that the shotgun He's given you is more than your little body can carry. It will be. He is doing this for some good reasons. First of all, He wants you to lean on Him. He wants you to prop up whatever He's given you on His strong shoulders. This will teach you that *"You can do everything with the help of Christ."* But then, He also wants others to see what God is able to do with someone who is willing to put their weakness into the hands of a strong God. Remember, if you can do it on your own, you won't need God. He will always call you to something that is bigger than yourself.

Prayer: "Father, teach my son that with You he can do all things."

Get Wisdom

James 1:[5]If you need wisdom—if you want to know what God wants you to do—ask him, and he will gladly tell you.

Proverbs 2:[1]My child, listen to me and treasure my instructions. [2]Tune your ears to wisdom, and concentrate on understanding. [3]Cry out for insight and understanding. [4]Search for them as you would for lost money or hidden treasure. [5]Then you will understand what it means to fear the LORD, and you will gain knowledge of God.

Son, in life you will need wisdom. Not very many have it these days. They have worldly wisdom, but not Godly wisdom. There is a difference. Wisdom is simply knowing how and when to apply what you know. Godly wisdom is based on what you know about God and His word. Worldly wisdom is based on knowledge that comes from the world. As a Christian, your knowledge for living needs to come from the Bible. And then you will need Godly wisdom to apply it.

This wisdom is so important because it will guide you down the right path. It will cause you to understand things around you from God's perspective. It will give you direction and allow you to make right decisions. The good thing about wisdom is it is a gift from God, but it is one that you must search for. I know this may be difficult to understand, so let me explain.

When you were young, your mother and I hid Easter eggs from you. We knew exactly where they were but didn't tell you. Instead, we let you find as many as you could. Eventually, if you couldn't find them all, we would give you clues and hints until you found every one. We were going to give them all to you but we were going to let you search as well. Without us you would have never found all of them, and yet you still searched.

God says that He *will* give you wisdom and that He *will not* withhold it from anyone. So how do we get it? First of all, you need to ask Him for it. This is what our first Bible verse talks about. Ask God and keep asking God. Make it a daily prayer. Next, search for it by learning God's word and living a life that puts God first. This is what the second Bible verse mentions. So, pray for wisdom, make God's word a priority, and faithfully follow God. And just when you think you are never going to find this wisdom, God will uncover it for you.

Prayer: "Lord, plant within my son a desire for Godly wisdom."

The True Measure of Success

Matthew 10:[42] "And if you give even a cup of cold water to one of the least of my followers, you will surely be rewarded."

Son, we both love all kinds of sports, especially basketball. I have played and coached much of my life. It is a great sport where only five get to play at any one time. You have also had many coaches and each has his own style and ability. You have had a good relationship with all of them.

As you know, coaches may ask you to do different things during a game. It may be to set a pick, run a certain play, or even shoot. Your job has been simply to do whatever the coach asks of you. At the end of the game, you have either won or lost. But winning or losing isn't the test of success. The test of success is did you do what the coach asked you to do. If you did, you were successful. Some games you might score a lot of points and some games none, but neither determines success; only did you do what you were asked to do. You may be disappointed at times but you must learn how to measure success this way.

In your Christian life, it will be measured this way as well. God may ask you to speak to thousands on one night and to give someone a cup of cold water the next day. Neither of these is more important than the other because both opportunities came from God. Success will be measured according to your obedience in both. This means that the size of your ministry will not mean anything to God. It also means that success will be measured day by day and even moment by moment. Remember that the true test of success for you will be if you are able to lie down at night and say to your Heavenly Father, "Father, I was successful today because I did exactly what you asked me to do."

Prayer: "Father, give my son many successes, as he follows You day by day."

Giving Your Best

> *Ecclesiastes 9:[10] Whatever you do, do well. For when you go to the grave, there will be no work or planning or knowledge or wisdom.*

Son, let's get something straight. I like to win and you should too. There is nothing wrong with competition and the last thing I want to see is you not giving your best. This really paints a wrong picture of the Christian life. Being a Christian does not mean that you are weak and that you let everyone run over you. The truth is Christians ought to lead out in being the very best at everything. There is nothing wrong with sitting on the bench, unless you are there because you have not competed with all that you have.

The Bible verse for today was my theme when I played basketball in high school. I determined that God would get the greatest glory if I played "well." Another Bible translation puts it this way. *"Whatever your hand finds to do, do it with your might."(NKJV)* I like that! Do it with your might! There is nothing that God despises more than one of His children doing something half-hearted. You are the child of God – the child of a King. He has all power and has given you that same power through His Holy Spirit. He gave the very best that He had when He gave His Son.

And if He gave His very best, the very least that you can do, is give that same best at everything you do.

So no matter if it is on a basketball floor, digging a ditch, at work, at church, or with your family; be the best!

Prayer: "Lord, remind my son that You gave Your best. Give him the desire to give his best as well."

A Resurrection

I Thessalonians 4: [13]*And now, brothers and sisters, I want you to know what will happen to the Christians who have died so you will not be full of sorrow like people who have no hope.* [14]*For since we believe that Jesus died and was raised to life again, we also believe that when Jesus comes, God will bring back with Jesus all the Christians who have died.*

Son, every creation of God was with purpose. Every part of nature will tell you something about God if you will look for it and ask Him to reveal it to you. One of the greatest pictures that God gives us in nature is the picture of death and a resurrection. A resurrection simply means that one day God will raise those who are dead and give them a new body and a new life. God wants all of us to know that our life on earth is not the end. Death for Christians is merely a change from life here, to life in Heaven. The Bible calls it "sleep" for those who are in Christ. Creation points to this truth.

Each night, you close your eyes to go to sleep. This pictures death. In the morning, your eyes open again, picturing a resurrection. The sun goes down each evening, picturing death. It comes up in the morning, picturing a resurrection. The leaves fall off of the trees in the fall and winter, picturing death. The trees produce new leaves in the spring, picturing a resurrection. This will be helpful to you as you grow older. It will give you a different point of view when you see someone die. It will let you know that God has taken something as sad as death and made good come out of it. And it will also give you comfort to know that your loved ones who have died may not be living here, but they are living in another place.

Prayer: "Lord, give my son Your viewpoint of death."

Becoming a Man

I Kings 2: [1]As the time of King David's death approached, he gave this charge to his son Solomon: [2]"I am going where everyone on earth must someday go. Take courage and be a man. [3]Observe the requirements of the LORD your God and follow all his ways. Keep each of the laws, commands, regulations, and stipulations written in the Law of Moses so that you will be successful in all you do and wherever you go.

Son, I can remember buying my first shotgun when I was sixteen years old. Those days were much different from today. No one thought I was a troubled young man or was concerned about what I might do with that gun. No, every young man either had one or wanted one. I can remember leaving that department store feeling as if I had reached manhood. It was one of the most memorable days of my life. My dad cautioned me about safety but thought nothing else about my purchase.

I know that you too have enjoyed the ownership of guns. I bought you your first new one when you were only ten. You will probably have it the rest of your life and then hand it down to your son.

Even though I felt like a full grown man when I bought my first shotgun; in reality, that did not make me a man. And it does not make you one either. Being a man means that you understand some big responsibilities. It means that you understand that sometimes you have to do what's right instead of what's best or instead of what you may want to do. It means understanding that others depend on you, are looking at you, and that you are willing to take on the role of being a good example. I can tell you are becoming that person and I am very proud of you.

It does take belongings to learn some of the qualities of being a man. And since you are going to own some things anyway, a gun is a great investment in your character and in your collection.

Prayer: "Father, my boy is becoming a man. Make him one that You are proud of."

Beating the Devil

Proverbs 17:[22]A cheerful heart is good medicine, but a broken spirit saps a person's strength.

Son, as you grow older, life will take on many responsibilities. You will go to work, get married, have children, and serve God. All of these things are serious subjects. They will add to your life a wealth of pleasure and also some heartache. Each of these can cause you to forget to have fun and laugh. Don't let that happen. Listen closely to what I am about to tell you.

You beat the devil! You are a Christian and have a home waiting for you in Heaven. Heaven will have no pain, heartache, or burdens. This means your time on earth will be as bad as it ever gets for you. Why not try to beat the devil here as well? You can if you choose to. Here's how. First of all, choose to be positive. Trouble is a fact of life. Don't think about how you will act *if* it comes. Instead, decide how you will react *when* it comes. It will come, but you can choose to not let the devil steal your attitude. You will beat him this way. Secondly, never stop having fun, and laugh. Find ways to play. Again remember, you have already beaten the devil in the next life. You want to beat him here as well. Now that you are a Christian, he can no longer do anything to you that

God does not allow. He answers to *your* Heavenly Father! Make time to hunt and fish. Make time for friends. Make time for your wife and children. Laugh at each other and yourself. This will be health for your mind, body, and spirit. And you can do this by simply deciding to. It doesn't take skill, talent, possessions or anything else other than a mind that is determined to not let the devil steal your joy.

Prayer: "Father, thank You that you have given my son everything he needs to defeat the devil in Heaven and on earth."

Get Prepared

Ephesians 6: 13 Use every piece of God's armor to
resist the enemy in the time of evil, so that after the
battle you will still be standing firm. 14 Stand your
ground, putting on the sturdy belt of truth and
the body armor of God's righteousness. 15 For shoes,
put on the peace that comes from the Good News,
so that you will be fully prepared. 16 In every battle
you will need faith as your shield to stop the fiery
arrows aimed at you by Satan. 17 Put on salvation
as your helmet, and take the sword of the Spirit,
which is the word of God. 18 Pray at all times and
on every occasion in the power of the Holy Spirit.

Son, hunting takes preparation, especially during the winter months. What you wear will make the difference as to whether you will be able to endure the cold or not.

Even now, I have to show you how to dress to stay warm. There is a method in what you put on. It matters what you have next to your skin, what you have as a middle layer, and what kind of insulation you have on to cover it all. And if your feet get cold early, you have already lost the battle. But once you have taken every provision to be prepared, it's time to hunt. It would be useless to have all the necessary things in order to hunt comfortably and then not go.

In the Christian life there is also a covering that you are to put on. It's called the armor of God. It is given to you in order that you might defeat satan and so that you can move forward in your Christian life. This armor will be everything you will ever need to be prepared and to have spiritual success. It is complete for your protection and for your progress. It includes the helmet of salvation, the belt of truth, the body armor of righteousness, the shoes of the good news of Jesus, and the shield of faith. Your weapon for progress is the sword of the word of God. But notice there is no protection for your back. God says that after you put on this armor, you are to stand. This is not to say there is never a time to retreat and regroup, but to not stand, would be like getting prepared to hunt and never going. You can't turn back now. His last word is to pray. Praying puts all of God's power with you. Remember, if God is for you, who can really stand against you? Nobody! This will be your daily covering the rest of your life. Get up each morning and ask God to get you ready.

Prayer: "Father, give my son protection and progress as he puts on Your armor."

You Have a Purpose

Psalm 139: [15] You watched me as I was being formed in utter seclusion, as I was woven together in the dark of the womb.[16] You saw me before I was born. Every day of my life was recorded in your book. Every moment was laid out before a single day had passed.[17] How precious are your thoughts about me, O God! They are innumerable!

Son, God has created you for a purpose. He is getting you ready even now for what He has in store for you. It will be great! And I promise you will love it. You see, God made us all special and for a special reason. He has a plan for your life and the sooner you realize it, the sooner He will be able to carry it out. He will not hide it from you even though you may not really discover it for a while. It will involve your dreams, talents, gifts and things you really like. Your childhood and youth years are real important. God doesn't just let children do what they want until they become adults. No,

He begins planting dreams and desires in your heart right now. These will serve as foundations for what He is calling you to do. Sometimes little things are such a part of our life we don't ever think that God could actually use something this simple. But He does.

As you begin this search, ask yourself what you love. Look at the areas He has gifted you in. Notice what talents you may have. These were all put there by God Himself. That doesn't mean they won't need to be developed, because they will. But God will work through that process as well. You see, the greatest basketball player always had the gift, but that doesn't mean that he didn't have to learn the right skills and practice a lot. Even so, you will have to do the same. God has already given you all you will ever need to do what He has called you to do. The next several years, and even the rest of your life, He will be developing you to be the very best at what He has purposed for your life. I'm excited for you and know that as you grow in your Christian life, you will become more than you will ever dream.

Prayer: "Father, thank You that You have a special plan for my son. Let him discover it early in life."

The Benefits of a Book

Exodus 24:[7] "Then he took the Book of the Covenant and read it to the people. They all responded again, "We will do everything the LORD has commanded. We will obey."

Son, until my late teenage years, I hated to read. It seemed that what my teachers wanted me to read was too boring. I'm not sure if it was, because I hardly ever read any of it. My fault. Today I love to read. It's true that reading is "fun"damental. It is both fun and essential to learning and growing.

One of my favorite places to read is in the deer stand on an afternoon hunt. It seems that the deer don't move until close to dark, so it's a perfect time for me to complete a good book. I also like reading on an airplane. I've found most people are not too interested in talking so I always bring something to read. I've read a lot of good books in these two places.

I know that reading is not high on your list of things to do right now but it is absolutely essential that you do this. It will be food for your soul and spirit, and for just general knowledge. That's why I like to read hunting and fishing magazines and Sports Illustrated as well.

Once you start reading you will discover its worth. You will learn things about life and about yourself that you would never otherwise learn. Start with your Bible. It's good to read a chapter or two each day. The book of Psalms is always encouraging for me. Also read Christian books. The Lord has gifted several good writers and you will settle on the ones you really like. During the most difficult times of your life, you will find the answers you need as you read the Bible and good Christian books. You will need faith during these times. It will come as you know more and more of the word of God. Trust me on this one, as one who also hated to read when I was your age.

Prayer: "Father, teach my son the benefits of Your Book and other good books as well."

Dedicated to the Lord

I Samuel 1:[26]"Sir, do you remember me?" Hannah asked. "I am the woman who stood here several years ago praying to the LORD. [27]I asked the LORD to give me this child, and he has given me my request. [28]Now I am giving him to the LORD, and he will belong to the LORD his whole life." And they worshiped the LORD there.

Son, when you were just born, your mother and I dedicated you to the Lord. It was a beautiful church service where we committed to raise you in a Christian home and allow God to do with you whatever He chose. I must admit that I didn't realize how hard that would be for me on occasion. All through your young life I have watched you play basketball. I always wanted you to score a lot of points, win the game on a last second shot, be the Most Valuable Player, lead the cheerleading squad, and sell popcorn all at the same time. Well, all dads do. Needless to say, it didn't always happen like I planned.

Sometimes you went through long slumps. It was during those times that I felt the pressure to pray, fast, and cry out to God for you. I think I even sinned because I worried about you. It was during those times God would always remind me of the day I gave you to Him. He would let me know that you are His, He knows what's best, and I just need to trust Him. That was a hard pill to swallow, but I agreed. I found myself falling into this same trap a few times over the years only to be reminded each time of Whose you really are. I'm still not perfect at this, but I'm growing each time.

Even though I take you back from God on occasion, the truth is, you *are* His. He does know better than I do and there's no doubt that He wants the very, very best for you, and *will* accomplish His plans for you.

Not only do I need to be reminded of this, you do to. You are His and when things don't go like you hoped they would, remind yourself that God has a plan even in something as small as missing a few shots. During those times, praise God anyway and not only will you beat discouragement, you will let God know that you understand that you are in good hands – even if they are not mine.

Prayer: "Father, my son was dedicated to You. Help us both never try to take him back."

Handling Success

Deuteronomy 8: 11"But that is the time to be
careful! Beware that in your plenty you do not
forget the LORD your God and disobey his
commands, regulations, and laws. 12For when you
have become full and prosperous and have built
fine homes to live in, 13and when your flocks and
herds have become very large and your silver and
gold have multiplied along with everything else,
14that is the time to be careful. Do not become proud
at that time and forget the LORD your God, who
rescued you from slavery in the land of Egypt. 15Do
not forget that he led you through the great and
terrifying wilderness with poisonous snakes and
scorpions, where it was so hot and dry. He gave you
water from the rock! 16He fed you with manna in
the wilderness, a food unknown to your ancestors.
He did this to humble you and test you for your
own good. 17He did it so you would never think
that it was your own strength and energy that
made you wealthy. 18Always remember that it is the
LORD your God who gives you power to become
rich, and he does it to fulfill the covenant he made
with your ancestors.

Son, I hope you have much success in this life. I pray that God blesses you with health and prosperity. I hope you are able to buy some nice things for yourself and others.

God's desire is to bless you with what you can handle, but most people can't handle success.

Over the years I've watched success cause most to forget God. You see, when things don't go so well, they turn to God for help. They cry out to Him to meet their needs, to get them through the problems they are going through, and to give them direction when they don't know what to do. They draw close to God through difficult times. On the other hand, when their life is going well, they have a lot of money in their pocket, and everything is falling into place, they forget about God. They no longer spend time with him in prayer, or go to church, and the humility they once had before God, has now turned to pride. Many times, God will have to take these things from them in order for them to return to Him.

One of the most difficult things you will need to do is continue to draw close to God through seasons of success. Make all of your successes move you to be more thankful, more humble, more giving, and have a greater desire to be alone with God. If you can do this, God will continue to give you even greater successes. If you can't, God may take these things from you, in order that you might draw near to Him. God's greatest desire is that you have a wonderful relationship with Him. Anything that keeps that from happening is standing between you and God.

Prayer: "Father, teach my son to draw close to You during tough times and closer during successful ones."

The Vine and the Branches

John 15:[4]Remain in me, and I will remain in you. For a branch cannot produce fruit if it is severed from the vine, and you cannot be fruitful apart from me. [5]"Yes, I am the vine; you are the branches. Those who remain in me, and I in them, will produce much fruit. For apart from me you can do nothing.

Son, you have worked hard at gaining some abilities in basketball. It has been a lifelong chase of yours to try to get better at your skills. In most ways, your effort has paid off. In other ways, you have seen how mistakes will still be made. As you grow older you will apply this same effort in other things as well. You will work hard to be the best father, husband, and worker. You will understand there are certain things demanded of you. When you have done these, you will be praised by those around you and will be blessed by all the rewards that come with it. In your Christian life, this is not how things work. You *cannot* live the Christian life. Let me say it again. You *cannot* live the Christian life! And God never expects you to.

If you spend your life trying to live up to all of the do's and don'ts in the Bible, you will get frustrated by all the times you are unable to do what you really want to do.

God's plan is this. Jesus will live out the Christian life in you, through the Holy Spirit. That is, you don't have to do anything but stay close to the Lord. If you will do that, He will do the work of getting the things into your life that He wants there, and getting out the things He wants to take out. Our scripture today illustrates this. Even though the branches hold the grapes, it is the vine that actually produces them. The branch simply "remains" in the vine. The branch stays connected to the vine, and holds the fruit that the vine is producing. That branch doesn't try real hard or worry over the fruit. It simply stays joined to the vine. You will have a great and joyful Christian life if you will learn now to remain close to the Lord and let Him live out His life through you. Staying close to God means that you have a relationship with Him, one that is like friends or one like we have. Our relationship would not be fun if you were just doing a bunch of rules that I commanded you to do. And as long as you are just trying to keep a bunch of rules for God, you will not have the kind of relationship He wants you to have with Him.

He loves you and He wants a relationship with you that is built on the real love you have for Him and the real love He has for you. If you will stay close to Him, He will bring it about.

Prayer: "Father, help my son understand early the joy of a real relationship with You."

Today

Matthew 6: [9]In this manner, therefore, pray: Our Father in heaven, Hallowed be Your name. [10]Your kingdom come, Your will be done On earth as it is in heaven.[11]Give us this day our daily bread. (NKJV)

Son, most of the things that will hinder you from doing all that God wants you to do and from being all that God wants you to be, will either come from your past or your future. Most will not come from the present. The devil will use your past to remind you of the times you failed and the mistakes that you have made. He will use the future to point out all of the obstacles that are in your way. He will cause them to look bigger than they are.

You must remember the past is only there to learn from and to be reminded of all the times that God has been faithful to you. The future is there to give you hope in God's promises that He has for you in the days ahead. But God tells us to live in the present. In our Bible verse today, Jesus teaches us to pray for "our daily bread." He never tells us to pray for what we need for tomorrow, only today. God has promised to give you everything you need for today. Never let the past stop you from doing what God wants you to do today. And never let the future stop you from believing God can get you through any problem that may come about. Trust Him today. When tomorrow comes, it will then be called "today." Trust Him today. When next Tuesday comes, and you wake up, it will be called "today." Trust Him today.

A wise man once said, "Yesterday is history. Tomorrow is a mystery. Today is a gift. That's why they call it the present."

Prayer: "Father, I thank You that You have promised everything my son needs, one day at a time."

Sowing and Reaping

Galatians 6:[7] Don't be misled. Remember that you can't ignore God and get away with it. You will always reap what you sow! [8] Those who live only to satisfy their own sinful desires will harvest the consequences of decay and death. But those who live to please the Spirit will harvest everlasting life from the Spirit. [9] So don't get tired of doing what is good. Don't get discouraged and give up, for we will reap a harvest of blessing at the appropriate time.

Son, a garden is a great example of today's scripture. If you put a tomato plant into the ground today, you won't be able to pick the tomatoes from it tomorrow – or even next week. The same goes for beans or cucumbers or anything that comes from our garden. If you plant today, you will not reap the harvest until later. At the same time, remember that you will also harvest more than you plant. Again, if you plant one tomato plant it is likely to produce more than a dozen tomatoes during the year. You will reap more than you sow.

This is a very important lesson to learn as you grow up. The things that you sow in your life today will be reaped in the future. This means all the decisions you make as a young person, will have an effect on your life as an adult. It may seem sometimes that you are not getting anything from going to church or reading your Bible or even praying. But you must remember that you never reap the same time as you plant.

You also need to be reminded that this also goes for bad decisions. It may seem that you will get by with doing things the wrong way or with disobeying God, but again, what we do now, we will pay for later. And remember, not only will we reap what we sow but more than we sow. So make sure you know how important it is to do what's right now. It will have a lasting effect on the adult you will become one day.

Prayer: "Father, I pray that my son will learn the truth of reaping and sowing, so he will be both pleasing to You and me."

Learning to Give

I Chronicles 29: [12]*Riches and honor come from you alone, for you rule over everything. Power and might are in your hand, and it is at your discretion that people are made great and given strength.* [13]*O our God, we thank you and praise your glorious name!* [14]*But who am I, and who are my people, that we could give anything to you? Everything we have has come from you, and we give you only what you have already given us!*

Son, I have already bought you a few guns over the years. Each one is unique and has a special purpose. On occasion I have used one of them on my own hunting trip. You never complained. Let's note some things about that gun of yours. First of all, I bought it for you. You had no money. Secondly, if I wanted my own I could buy it, but I like borrowing yours. And thirdly, I'm bigger than you are and if I wanted to take it from you, I could. Now why am I telling you this? Because this is how you will do God if you don't give a portion of your money to Him through your church and other ministries.

How silly it is to refuse to give up something that actually comes from God anyway? And He *is* bigger than both of us. If He wants it bad enough, He can just take it. So why does He chose to borrow the money that He has given us? It is because He wants us to always be reminded that it is God who gives us all the good things in our life. He wants us to understand that money is not how we get things, God is. And He also wants to build in us a greater trust in Himself.

Each time you put your money in an offering plate you should thank God for all He has given you and remind yourself that money is not really what you need in life – God is. And since He owns everything, you will never have to wonder if you are giving too much. He will never let you give more to Him than He will give back to you.

Prayer: "Father, teach my son that giving will build his trust in You."

Build an Altar

Genesis 12:[7] Then the LORD appeared to Abram and said, "I am going to give this land to your offspring." And Abram built an altar there to commemorate the LORD'S visit.

Son, boys are good at building things. They are also good at tearing things apart, but we will talk about that another time. I think every man would love to be able to be a good handy man. We love tools. I have tools that I don't even know what they do. But I've got em', and you will too. One of the things that you will need to learn to build is an altar. Let me explain.

In the Old Testament, when God spoke to one of His people, that individual always built an altar. Abraham, Isaac, Jacob, and Moses were some of the men who built altars. They built them to remind themselves and others where and when the Lord spoke to them. And they didn't build just one; they built them as often as the Lord spoke. These altars were solid reminders of exactly what God had told them. They needed these reminders during times of doubt.

God will speak to you many, many times in your life if you will let Him. He will speak very clearly but what He tells you now may not take place for days, months, or years. Doubt will try to tell you that God never spoke or that you did not hear Him correctly. That is why it is important to build an altar each time God speaks to you about something specific. Now, our altars today don't have to be of wood and nails (they can be), but they can be something as simple as keeping a written record of the day and time that God spoke. We call them journals. But anything can be used in order for you to be reminded of God's clear words to you. I've even taken my pocket knife and carved a letter in a tree. It doesn't matter what it is. Just make sure that you are building altars so you will always be able to go back to them and remind yourself of God's words to you.

Prayer: "Lord, teach my son the value of being reminded of Your words to him."

Thinking Rightly

Romans 12:[2]Don't copy the behavior and customs of this world, but let God transform you into a new person by changing the way you think. Then you will know what God wants you to do, and you will know how good and pleasing and perfect his will really is.

Son, I can only remember getting into one fight when I was young. I can't remember what we fought about but only that I was real nervous and because others were watching, I had to fight. It only lasted a few seconds before the other guy gave up. I was the winner without every getting close to the other guy's face. I look back at that fifth grade experience now and laugh at how silly we both must have looked.

It seems that boys want to fight more than girls, but every person fights battles. But the battles that we all constantly fight are not physical ones but emotional and spiritual ones. These will be the battles that you will fight as well. What you will need to understand is the battle will always take place in your mind. Not sometimes, but always. If the devil can get you thinking wrongly, he will be able to get you to act wrongly. Remember, right actions always follow right thoughts and wrong actions always follow wrong thoughts. That's why it is extremely important that you learn the Scriptures. That way, they are in your mind. And if they are in your mind they will determine your actions.

When a thought comes into your mind always weigh it against the Bible to see if it's a good thought or a bad thought. For instance, you may wake up one morning and the thought comes into your mind that God doesn't love you. That thought may come to you because of something you did or didn't do. But when you look at the Bible, it says *"For God so loved the world that He gave His only begotten Son."* This means that the thought that God doesn't love you must not be coming from God but from the devil. You are then to speak the truth – and do it out loud; so that the untrue thought is replaced by the true one. So you see why it will be important for you to know and keep learning the truth of the word of God. That's why church attendance, Sunday School, and discipleship classes are important. And that is also why you should study the Bible on your own. You must know the word of God. It is the sword of the Spirit that will help you win the battle of the mind.

Prayer: "Father, give my son a desire to know your Word, so that he might win the battles that will be fought in the mind."

Your New Identity

II Corinthians 5: [17] *Therefore, if anyone is in Christ, he is a new creation; old things have passed away; behold, all things have become new. (NKJV)*

Son, it was a real thrill for your mother and me when you decided to give your heart and life to Christ. Our whole family will now be together in Heaven.

When God saved you He changed you. He did not make you a better person. He made you a new person. He did not remodel your house. He completely tore it down and put up a new one. The Bible says the old you, (before you were saved) is dead and now there is a new you. You have a new identity. You have a new family. According to the Bible, you were once in the family of sinners but now you are in the family of saints. A saint is simply a child of God. That doesn't mean that you are not going to sin but it means that sinning goes against who you are now as a member of a new family. This is important to know because who you think you are will influence what you do. Let me give you an example.

If you were to constantly say, "I'm a thief, I'm a thief, I'm a thief;" you would always be more tempted to steal. Your identity would be that of a thief. Also, if a father always tells his son that he is worthless, no good, and will never amount to anything, his identity will be that of someone who is all of these things. Your new identity in Christ says this about you. You are God's exceptional creation. You have a great purpose. Jesus so loves you that He died for you. Through Him there is nothing that you can't do. He will never leave you and He promises that no matter how many times you mess up, He will always welcome you back to Him. This means that just as you are special to me as a part of my family, you are even more special to Him as a part of the family of God. Even though you may love sports or hunting and fishing, these do not describe who you are. You are, and will always be, a son.....mine and God's. Always remember this and you will act in a way that is pleasing to both.

Prayer: "Father, always remind my son that You have made him new, and that he is now Your child."

Putting First Things First

Daniel 6: [10]But when Daniel learned that the law had been signed, he went home and knelt down as usual in his upstairs room, with its windows open toward Jerusalem. He prayed three times a day, just as he had always done, giving thanks to his God.

Son, as you get older, time will become more valuable to you. You will have to manage it according to the things that are most important. If you truly want your faith to be at the top of your list you will have to give it some time. That doesn't mean you are only going to church but it means that you are making room for your faith to grow each day by spending time alone with God. It may be in the morning or before bedtime, but if you do not plan this time, you will not give it its rightful place.

At first, the devil will try to convince you that nothing is being accomplished and that you could be doing something more useful. But if you will continue to meet God during these periods, you will understand how important this time really is.

When you have your time with God, come with your Bible, a devotional book, a notebook, and a pen. These will be the tools that will keep you on target. Read a devotional from your book each day. Also read a part of the Scriptures.........and read a chapter of the Psalms everyday. Your notebook and pen will serve several purposes. You can write down what and who you want to pray for and for answered prayer. You can also use your notebook like a diary. Today we call it a journal. A journal is simply a book where you write down anything that is going on in your life and even what you are thinking about. This journal will allow you to look back one day and see just how God was directing your thoughts and actions. It will also be an encouraging reminder that God is faithful.

Don't think that you can just squeeze this activity in some part of each day. You must plan for it. If you do this, I promise that your life will be more than you could have ever imagined. You will have God's direction everyday. You will know His plans for you. But the greatest thing about these times with Him will be the peace of mind that you *will* have and the worry that you *won't* have. If you will do this one thing, all other parts of your life will fall in place.

Prayer: "Father, teach my son early how important it is to spend time with You."

Superstitions

Philippians 4:[13]For I can do everything with the help of Christ who gives me the strength I need.

Son, each sport has its own unique skills that it takes to perform. The best athletes are gifted with a special ability and with a love for their particular sport. These things can only come from God. For these athletes to become the best, they have had to spend their whole life mastering just one thing. Whether they win or not is also in the hands of God and in their own willingness to train. That is one reason I don't like seeing ball players holding on to superstitions.

Baseball players have plenty of them. They might only wear a certain hat on game day or refuse to step on a base line. Other sports have players that will only eat certain things on the day of the game or may only wear certain colors. These are all superstitions. Superstition is putting faith in some object that you believe has some magical power over an outcome. For instance, when a baseball pitcher refuses to step on the white base line, he is saying that he believes if he steps on that line something bad will happen. When he does this, he does two things. First, he lessens the value of all the time and work he has put in to become great. And two, he makes these his god. The Bible calls this idolatry and one form of idolatry is making an object a god that you pray to or put faith in.

As a Christian you must only put your faith for any outcome in the hands of God and in your own desire to be the best. Nothing else matters. Nothing else will determine the outcome of anything in life. That doesn't mean that you will be able to understand everything and that strange things won't happen, but it simply means that you must always remember God is in control. Our verse today says it all. You and God need nothing else.

Prayer: "Father, teach my son to depend only upon You."

It Takes Sacrifice

I Chronicles 21: "[22]David said to Araunah, "Let me buy this threshing floor from you at its full price. Then I will build an altar to the LORD there, so that he will stop the plague."

[23]"Take it, my LORD, and use it as you wish," Araunah said to David. "Here are oxen for the burnt offerings, and you can use the threshing tools for wood to build a fire on the altar. And take the wheat for the grain offering. I will give it all to you."

[24]But the king replied to Araunah, "No, I insist on paying what it is worth. I cannot take what is yours and give it to the LORD. I will not offer a burnt offering that has cost me nothing!"

Son, some of the best hunts I can remember were when I had to overcome certain conditions or go through extreme measures to kill a deer or turkey. Most of the time the difficulty came from the weather conditions. I have hunted in the extreme cold, the rain-flooded, and even severe windy conditions. I have slithered on my stomach to get close enough to an animal. I have climbed steep mountains and crawled out of even steeper hollows. At the end of each hunt, I was glad that I did – whether I came out with an animal or not.

Many times I have found that success only comes when I'm willing to go beyond what others are prepared to do. It comes when I'm willing to sacrifice the easy for the difficult.

The best things in your life will come with great sacrifice. You have learned that through basketball. There are not many who are willing to put in the individual time to become better. You will be tempted your entire life to take the easy road, to hunt close to your truck; to fish easily reachable pools. Sometimes that will be all you have to do in order to bring home a mess of fish, but the best trophies will come only if you are willing to sacrifice to get them.

What goes for hunting, fishing, and sports, also goes for your home, work, and spiritual life. You can get there by taking the easy road that most people are on, but the road less traveled will hold the best rewards that only a few will ever know and enjoy. It may cost you something but that is what sacrifice is all about.

Prayer: "Lord, help my son not only see the cost of sacrifice, but also its benefits."

Don't Be a Workaholic

Matthew 6:[33]But seek first the kingdom of God and His righteousness, and all these things shall be added to you.

Son, it seems today that being a workaholic is something to be proud of. A workaholic is someone who works all the time. This word is especially used when it comes to describing coaches. A coach who is just hired will say, "No one will outwork me." They are quick to tell stories of how they rarely go home and sleep on a couch in their office. Their hope is they will be perceived as someone who will do more than anyone else. They are also of the belief there is no other way to win. As a result of the endless days and nights they work, many of them have ignored their spouse and their children. And some families have split apart.

What I want to tell you is this......... don't let work, the desire for money and power, or the desire to win, cause you to neglect your family. They may say they understand, but they don't. Just because someone works longer and harder doesn't mean they are guaranteed to be successful. God doesn't want you to neglect your faith and family for any job. He will bless what you do when you put the most important things first. You can be sure that if you will put your faith and your family first, God will make your work-life successful. It is better to work forty hours with God on your side than fifty outside of His will. Remember that God will help you accomplish more than all others when you put the things of God in their rightful place. Don't fall into the trap of the world. Tell them upfront what is important to you. If you don't you might be sleeping on the couch even when you don't want to.

Prayer: "Father, never let my son be a workaholic at the expense of his faith and family."

Tell Someone

Psalm 71:[24]I will tell about your righteous deeds all day long.

Son, most of us men don't like to get our picture taken unless we are holding a fish or standing beside a row of ducks that we have just shot. I really don't know why other than we have to dress up and we can't wear our hat. But when it comes to fish, fowl, or an animal, we not only want our picture taken, we want to show it to everyone. Right now in my truck, I have one of me and a wild hog just in case I run into someone that hasn't yet heard my story. Pictures are our way of sharing a great experience with someone else. They give us an opportunity to tell the story of what happened. When we tell others our story, it helps us to relive the event ourselves and gives others encouragement for their own adventures.

In the same way, you must always be eager to share the story of your Christian life with others as well. Your life is to be the picture that others see. This picture ought to show what living for Christ is all about. But a picture is not as good without the story. When you tell someone about the goodness of God and how Christ changed you, you are not only reminding yourself of how God saved you, but you are giving them the good news that God can save them too. That's why it is important that the picture they see in you goes along with the story you are telling. When God is living His life through you it will be easy to tell others about His goodness. It is good to live it. It is also good to tell it. But it is best to live it and tell it.

Prayer: "Father, let my son never be ashamed to tell others about You."

Learn to Pray

I Samuel 3:[9] So he said to Samuel, "Go and lie down again, and if someone calls again, say, 'Yes, LORD, your servant is listening.'" So Samuel went back to bed.[10] And the LORD came and called as before, "Samuel! Samuel!" And Samuel replied, "Yes, your servant is listening."

Son, you will be successful in most areas of life if you will learn to communicate. All of your relationships will either grow or die according to whether you communicate or not. To communicate simply means that you are having conversation with someone else or some group that you have something in common with. Remember also that communication is not only one person doing the talking but it is two or more.

Now if you and I never talked, we would not have a good relationship. Or if when we got together, I did all of the talking, that also would not be a healthy relationship. This not only goes for you and me, but it goes for husband and wife, parents and children, coaches and players, employees and employers, and especially God and us.

Prayer is how we communicate with God. But it is not just about us talking to Him and telling Him all that we want Him to do, it is about allowing Him to speak to us as well. This is where many people mess up. Their prayer time is made up of them doing all of the talking, saying "Amen," and then leaving. They leave no time for God to speak to them. You cannot be this way. You must give God time to speak to you. And no matter what you see on TV, God does speak to His children. He will do this as you think on the Scriptures and allow the Holy Spirit to guide those thoughts. As you can see, this takes more time than just getting up after you have told God what you want Him to do.

The reason most people do not have a healthy relationship with God is because they never give God time to speak to them. Their communication only involves them talking to God and not God talking to them. If you will apply this truth to your life, all of your relationships will be healthy, especially your relationship with God.

Prayer: "Father, speak to my son early in his life, so that he will know the value of communicating with You."

Being Rejected

Hebrews 10: [35]*Do not throw away this confident trust in the Lord, no matter what happens. Remember the great reward it brings you!* [36]*Patient endurance is what you need now, so you will continue to do God's will. Then you will receive all that he has promised.*

Son, always be a dreamer. Nothing in this life was every accomplished or invented without someone first having a dream. Dreams are from God if they don't go against the Bible. Remember this and you will find your purpose for life. Your dreams will always be bigger than you can accomplish in your own power. God makes them that way in order for you to look to Him and call to Him as you pursue those dreams. You must also know that following those dreams will be hard. If it was easy, everybody would be doing it.

Perhaps the most difficult thing about accomplishing great things is facing rejection. Rejection means hearing "no" a lot. Some people will let this rejection cause them eventually to quit. The "no's" will become so frequent that discouragement will follow and finally they will let go of the dream they were pursuing. If you will make sure your dream is from God, you will be able to outlast any rejection that you might get. If you know you are pursuing that which God wants you to pursue, you will come to realize that rejections are just God's tools that keeps you on the right path, headed to the place where you will hear a loud "YES!"

Prayer: "Father, give my son the strength to keep following the dreams You have given him even when he faces rejection."

You Must Live By Faith

Romans 4:[18] When God promised Abraham that he would become the father of many nations, Abraham believed him. God had also said, "Your descendants will be as numerous as the stars," even though such a promise seemed utterly impossible! [19] And Abraham's faith did not weaken, even though he knew that he was too old to be a father at the age of one hundred and that Sarah, his wife, had never been able to have children.[20] Abraham never wavered in believing God's promise. In fact, his faith grew stronger, and in this he brought glory to God. [21] He was absolutely convinced that God was able to do anything he promised. [22] And because of Abraham's faith, God declared him to be righteous.

Son, the life of a Christian is to be lived by faith. As you grow spiritually, you will learn more about what it means to live this lifestyle. But since it is so important I must mention it now. Faith is so crucial to your life that the Bible says, *"Without faith it is impossible to please God."(Heb 11:6 NKJV)* So if you are not walking by faith you are not pleasing God. Living by faith means that I am trusting God through a growing, love relationship so that my life gives evidence of things only God can do. This doesn't mean that you don't have to get a job, but it means that you understand it is God who provides a job. It also means that you allow God to be your guide throughout each day. Sometimes this is easy, other times it is real difficult. For instance, if God leads you to give someone $25.00, that might be easy, but if God leads you to give $2500.00, that will be hard.

Living by faith is coming to the conclusion that it was God that led you to do something, and then doing it no matter how impossible it may seem (like Abraham). Never forget what I am about to tell you. As you grow in your Christian life, God will eventually ask you to do some things that seem impossible for you to do. He did it all through the Bible and He still does it. This is the only way that God gets glory. If we live our lives doing things within our own power, we get the glory. If the impossible is done, only God can get the glory. This lifestyle is not for a select few, it is for every child of God. Learn this and you will see God do things through your life that you could never do on you own. Yes, at times it will be difficult, but as you see God do what He says He will do, you will be able to follow Him the next time He leads you back into the land of the impossible.

Prayer: "Father, build my son's faith now so it will be strong in the future."

Finally

Son, life can become very difficult at times. There will be days that you will be overwhelmed by all the things that are in your life. It will be at those times that perhaps you will go back and pick up this little book and turn to a certain lesson that applies to the situation that you are going through at that time. Keep it close, but remember that it only points to your real source of hope and help, and that is your Heavenly Father who is revealed in the Bible. Come to know the Scriptures and you will know God. Come to know God and you will know His Son. Come to know His Son and you will know His Spirit. Come to know His Spirit and you will have all the strength you will ever need to face each day. This is not my promise, but His.

-Dad-

About the Author

Gary Miller writes to hunters and fishermen in a weekly column. He is a former pastor and is the founder of Outdoor Truths Ministries. He also speaks across the country to hunters and fishermen about faith and the outdoors. His own son, now 24 years old, played basketball in both NCAA division I and division II conferences. In the early years, while traveling with his son, Gary was able to share the lessons of life, while both shared their love for basketball, the outdoors, and sports of every kind.

For other books by Gary, visit www.outdoortruths.org

Made in the USA
Lexington, KY
02 February 2015